STRESS MANAGEMENT

Dr. Alfred Jones

STRESS CONTROL PRODUCTS LIMITED
93 New Road, Rubery, Birmingham B45 9JR
Tel: 021 453 1914   Telex 334225 Stesco G

Printed by Thomas Reed Printers Limited, Sunderland and London.

Foreword

I once heard a doctor say, "People don't kill themselves from over work, but they can kill themselves from over worry". What did he mean by this? To answer this question, we go directly to the heart of the matter regarding stress. Over the past several years I have come across some very excellent books and articles on stress. Many of them are directed toward the executive, toward people in very responsible jobs. Once we understand what stress "is" and what it "is not" we will be in a better position to understand why stress is applicable to everyone of us — not just those at the top of the social ladder.

The most important thing about stress is that is has absolutely nothing to do with the here and now. Stress is always about the future. It is about something that we think **will** happen to us. Throughout this book, every time there is an example of people in a stressful situation, we will talk about a threat, a fear of some future experience. All of us are much stronger than we realize. We are capable of dealing with all aspects of our lives. What we can't quite seem to manage is the anticipated happening.

Stress has nothing to do with the here and now, it is about what we think, we fear, we anticipate will happen to us. This anticipated happening is so strong, so powerful that it completely engulfs us, completely controls us, completely overwhelms us. Once we learn to take control, we are on our way to learning how to let stress work for us rather than against us.

What then is stress? First of all, we used to think of it in terms of architecture. We talked about stress in relationship to the amount of energy needed to bend or break a piece of wood or steel. It was not until the last fifteen to twenty years that we began to understand what we are now calling "psychological stress". For the past fifty years, we began to suspect that many of our physical problems had an emotional or psychological basis. From study and research, an entirely new body of medicine came into being. It was called "psychosomatic" — the mind or feelings, or emotions were responsible for many, many actual physical illnesses.

Using this new concept as a stepping stone, we began to understand more about the end result of the "pressures" and the "stresses" that all of us were under much of the time. We began to see how it was that such things as depression, insomnia, headaches, fatigue, muscular tension, high blood pressure, work and study difficulties, excessive use of tobacco, alcohol and even over-eating could be the end result of stress. An entirely new concept was now open to us. We were able to think more about the "emotional" state of our health", about what doctors began to call "stressors" as we began to address many of these conditions.

With all of the new knowledge, with the new techniques that were beginning to be developed, it now became possible for people to do something about it. More and more, we were able to take responsibility for our own treatment. The world of "self help" began to take on more and more importance.

Doctors no longer write all of their prescriptions in Latin. People are no longer expected to do things just because someone told them to do so. We began to read, to think, to discuss and we are now very much a part of an enlightened society. This is a very good thing for two very important reasons. In the first place, we are an educated public, a public wanting to know more and more about how things work. Also, we are now beginning to understand that we are responsible for consequences. If we over do it, then we know why we suffer. We can't continue to go around blaming someone else.

Last year, I was asked to give a lecture to an audience of more than 100 people in an adult education class. Since my lecture was about stress, I was curious to know how the audience, people from many walks of life perceived stress. I therefore started off by sampling the feelings of the audience. One man said, "Stress is about the reactions of the managing director of a big company. You have a lot of problems to worry about". Another said, "I think air traffic controllers must have a stressful job". A young lady said that to her stress was what happened when you tried to cross a busy road when there was a lot of traffic. A very interesting comment came from an older woman who said, "stress, well if anyone in my family had stress I'd kick them up the backside". It became clear to me that people were certainly aware of the articles and stories we see in print today about stress, but in actual fact, did not really know very much about it. It was at that point that I began to realize that any endeavour regarding stress had to start with some very simple types of public education. This book, therefore, is what one might call Stress Education For Everyman — not just the managing director of a large company, indeed not just for the work force of that large company, but for people, young and old from every socio-economic strata from every walk of life.

In his book, LIFE AFTER STRESS Dr. Martin Shaffer gives us some examples of the type of stress that we experience in a typical day. He describes a scene which took place on a Friday afternoon only a half hour before the closing time at a bank. There were long queues of customers waiting to make deposits or withdraw money for the weekend. At one teller's window, a merchant steps forward and opens a bag with a stack of cheques and deposits almost two inches thick. This transaction will take at least ten minutes. There were three customers in the long queue, Gary, Mike and Ginny. First Gary noticed the man with the lengthy transaction. He was furious. He grinds out his cigarette and mutters to himself about inconsiderate people who wait until the last minute to transact their weekly banking. He shifts back and forth from foot to foot, experiencing more and more frustration. He searches his pocket for an antacid tablet, finding none, he curses under his breath and lights another cigarette.

Several places behind him is Mike. He has an important appointment shortly and he is concerned that he will be late. Unlike Gary, Mike works hard to cope with his irritation. He takes several deep breaths, reminds himself that there is nothing he can do about it and gazes out of the window focusing his attention upon the beautiful trees that line the street.

Directly behind Mike, Ginny is dealing with the situation in another way. Before she came into the bank, she knew that she might be in for a long and frustrating wait. She realized that it was late on a Friday afternoon so she made sure she had plenty of time to spend. She even brought along an Agatha Christie novel to occupy her time. She only vaguely noticed the merchant with the time-consuming amount of work. She adjusted her stance to feel more comfortable and continued reading.

All three of these people have been subjected to a typical stressful situation, not unlike the stresses each of us is subjected to each day. Each however, reacted in a dramatically different way. But why is this the case? Dr. Shaffer points out that people who know little about stress often assume that it is some kind of powerful force that is exerted on us. Gary assumes that it is someone elses fault, that he has no responsibility for what happens. Mike was more realistic and Ginny was not only able to anticipate what may happen, but was prepared to practice stress reduction behaviour. Gary did not just happen to feel stressed at the bank, his responses were the end result of a complex interaction among different aspects of his thought and behaviour. He had planned poorly. He arrived at the bank late on a

Friday incorrectly assuming that it would not take him long to transact his business. Add his fatigue at the end of a long week, his incessant smoking, many cups of coffee and you have a problem waiting to happen. His tendency to blame others for things that happen causes him to place himself in risk of becoming a stress sufferer.

Your stress control biofeedback card is the first step in helping you begin to fight back against stress. This really is the card you can't leave home without. People can't seem to keep thier hands off it. It is a relaxation trainer. It is a challenge to get it to turn blue. Although we will go into the actual development of the liquid crystal in Chapter 8, basically, the crystal is heat sensitive. When you are stressed, blood is drawn into the centre of your body, leaving your hands cold. When you place your thumb on the crystal, it will change colour as your relax. Initially, if you are stressed the crystal will remain black. When you are tense, it will turn red, but when you are calm, it is green and when you are very relaxed, it is blue.

People of all ages can use the card. It is very interesting to see small children use the card. Even at an early age, you can be taught what stress is all about and how your stress level can be controlled. Young people experience a great deal of stress during the adolescent years. A very stressful time in the lives of individuals occurs at the time of retirement. In other words, this book and stress programme is recommended for people of all ages. We hope that very soon every member of your family will have their personal biofeedback stress card.

Table of Contents

1

What is stress all about?

Man has always been subjected to it although we might not have always known as much about it as we do today. Certainly the 20th century brought with it new problems as we attempt to live in a rapidly moving industrial age. We believe that there are a greater variety of circumstances producing stress than man has experienced in past generations. At no time in the past have we seen so many physical illnesses that have had an emotional basis. Medical practitioners and scientists have now begun to study, research and learn more about the relationship to the unique features of our complicated society and the effects it has upon us. It is generally considered that there are far more cases of depression, anxiety, tension, difficulties in sleeping patterns, backache, headache, sluggishness, over eating, excessive smoking, excessive use of alcohol, problems of interpersonal relationships and general frustrations than have been experienced in past centuries. Science has kept pace in the development of instruments that can diagnose stress. The electrocardiograph for understanding more about the function of the heart is of great value in diagnosis. The electroencephlograph gives us valuable information about the brain. Other instruments measure galvanic skin response and temperature tell us more about the relationship between feelings, emotions and our physical bodies. With the development of microprocessors, electronics, and the integrated circuit, psychologists have had available to them biofeedback monitors that can measure many of the physical aspects of stress. We are now able to teach individuals how to recognize stress and its symptoms.

Almost every time I discuss stress, people ask me, "Isn't stress necessary for us to do our jobs?" "Isn't it true that some people thrive on stress?" The answer is without a doubt, "Yes, stress is not only necessary and helpful, but often a positive force." Then why do we talk about the stress epidemic? Why do we talk about stress as a killer? Like any powerful force in the universe, we need to understand it and to control it. I like to use the example of the gear box of an automobile. In order to get started we have to shift into first gear. It is very powerful and enables us to have maximum strength. But once we get going, the task is to be able to shift into fourth or fifth gear so that the car is operating most efficiently. If we drove it in first gear all day, we would soon burn out the gear box and damage the engine. Many people drive their bodies under stress all the time. They are without a doubt damaging themselves in the process. Stress control teaches us how to "shift into fifth gear" as it were, to operate more efficiently.

With more understanding of stress we can actually control many of the physical and psychological effects it has upon us. With this understanding and control, it will no longer cause so many of the painful stress symptoms. Once we are able to use stress to our advantage, we can use the energy that we previously used incorrectly so that we will now use stress to work for us. As a consequence, we will be able to devote far more engergy to undertaking the tasks at hand. Again with the illustration of the motorcar, in fifth gear we will not be using so much fuel.

Virtually every highly successful person in a variety of walks of life experiences a great deal of stress daily. It can often increase their motivation, their drive and their will to succeed. But, in others, stress completely controls them and they succumb to the unfortunate results that it brings with it.

There is a direct relationship between stress and many of the present day harmful behaviour patterns. With bio-feedback training as presented in Chapter 8, we can enable one to deal more effectively with stress. The task is to develop the ability to understand stress and to cope more effectively with it. Ultimately, we will be able to practice stress reduction automatically.

As we look at examples of stress as we experience it in our lives each day, we need to keep in mind the most important thing about stress. In an emotional sense, it has nothing to do with the here and now. Stress is about the future. It is about something we think will occur. Throughout the book, stress will be related to the word "threat". We anticipate that something of a threatening nature will occur. This is the primary factor in causing all of stress conditions that adversely affect us.

One of the most stressful things we do is to stand in a queue. We experience this at the post office, at the market, at the bank and even at the petrol station. There are varying degrees of reactions to standing in a queue. Frustration is one of them. Other people are slow, often the clerks are inefficient. We feel a knot in our stomach. We are in a hurry. If we are late, adverse things will happen. We need to get through the queue and on our way.

Some stressors are associated with the time of the year. The holidays, Christmas, Easter, etc. are very stressful. Often we worry because we have to spend money and we worry about what will happen if we do not have enough money. We worry about buying presents. Will we get something that people will like. Will they be happy or angry at us depending on what we get them. If we stop to think about it, we can remember many, many aspects of Christmas that can cause us to 'borrow problems for tomorrow'. As we anticipate our summer holidays, there are problems of a different variety, but problems none the less. Will the travel arrangements work out as we planned? Will our hotel reservations be to our liking? What will be happening at home while we are away? Again, will we have enough money?

Without a doubt there is stress associated with tax time. There is stress associated with any deadline. Students have to turn in papers. In the work place, reports have to be prepared. Always we are anticipating the worst. We are constantly worried about what will happen. We live in constant fear of the unknown. Fear that we will fail, fear that we will be criticized, fear that we will not be accepted is constantly with us.

Parents experience stress when their children are away from home. We experience stress about the condition of the weather. It is almost as if someone can name it and we will find someone who worries about it. This is stress. This is what stress is all about. It doesn't have to be that way. We can fight back, we can learn to let stress work for us rather than against us.

2

Physical Stress and Mental Stress

Although the conditions that precipitate stress that we experience in the 20th century are unique, the manner in which our bodies react are ancient. In past centuries, going back to the emergence of man, he had to face threat to his life almost daily. Nature was harsh and primitive man was cruel. Fight or flight was the watchword. Death was the rule not the exception. In the wild today, we see this exemplified in the animal kingdom. But for man, today, in a civilized sophisticated society, fight or flight is not the watchword. We have greater capacities to think, to reason, to communicate and we utilize logical processes and have a higher degree of intelligence and this makes us vastly different from our primitive ancestors. The ancient physical system whereby the body responds to conditions of threat has changed little, whereas the world in which man lives has been fundamentally altered. Living creatures change extremely slowly — adapted as they are to adjust to slow geological change. Our systems can not keep pace with the vast changes in our environment which came about with the rise of civilized societies with their complex social organization, inventiveness, techniques, speed of movement and information and methods of destruction. It has been said that our built in response systems are out of date, designed to meet the needs of man living in a primitive and now vanished world. It is this ancient physical system which is responsible for much of what we call the physical symptoms of stress, symptoms which we recognize as precursors of disease.

Dr. Ivor Pleydell-Pearce of Bristol University helps us to make a distinction between physiological stress and mental or psychological stress. He points out that over the millions of years, since we are all mortal and vulnerable, the body has built up very adequate defenses against danger or damage which is why we have lasted as long on this earth as we have. These defenses are really quite complex. You see them in every illness, you see them whenever the body is damaged or injured in any way. You see these defences being mustered when the body is attacked by virus or bacterial infection. When the body is attacked, it begins to assemble its natural defences. Information is passed out from the brain to all parts of the body associated with the defence reaction. For instance, information which stimulates part of the adrenal gland, called the medulla releases adrenalin into the blood stream. This has the effect of mobilizing the energy reserve of the body, utilizing stored sugar and diverting blood from the smooth muscles of the stomach to the striate muscles which are used for bodily movement so primitive man could fight or run away. This is a very normal and proper thing to happen. Hormones are also released and it is their task to build up a wall of inflammation between any damaged part of the body and the rest of it to keep bacteria and viruses out. This is a useful protective endeavour, but of course this should not be allowed to last too long for if it persists a considerable strain is placed on the defensive system and other parts of the body as well. It is of interest to point out that while this process is going on, in response to some physiological stressors, we become very vulnerable to secondary stressors. For example, in the case of a terminal illness such as cancer, death is often the result of pneumonia. Combatting the secondary illness under such circumstances is far more difficult. Again, it is good and proper that our defensive system be called into play when there is danger to the body. But the question arises, what will happen when you begin to experience these changes when you are under **psychological** or **emotional** stress. This then becomes inappropriate. It is one thing to have your body under attack, but having one's personal views attacked is another matter. It will be very helpful if we can understand why it is that under mental stress these same physical responses occur. You see, unlike physical stress, psychological stress doesn't necessarily get resolved. You therefore have an entrance into all of the stress diseases because these defences, if prolonged are the beginning of such problems as ulcers, heart disease, diabetes, and all of the various other conditions that occur when psychological stress continues.

Most of the world's researchers today agree that psychological stress starts with the key word "threat". What happens is that we **believe** that something is going to happen. We think that a problem will occur. It matters little whether or not this anticipated problem will actually occur. We **believe** that it will and this is reality for us. When we anticipate the worst, we respond according to how we have been programmed. If for example, we think that someone in our organization is after our job, the fact that they are not is unimportant. They may even care a great deal for you and only want your welfare, but if you think that they are after your job this is reality for you. Whenever an individual is threatened what he normally does is to perceive threat and attempt to cope with it. The way in which we cope with threats, real or imagined, is dependent on how we have been programmed.

During our lifetime, we have learned methods of coping with threat, that is to say, we have learned coping strategies. Some people tell lies, and this is the way in which they have learned or have been programmed to cope with situations that threaten them. Other people run away, others get angry and attack, but of course in the end if you can't deal with threat in that way and when your usual coping mechanisms fail to hold, you are on your way to becoming a stress sufferer. Remember, there are two very important things about psychological stress. In the first place it is not about the here and now, it is about the future. Secondly, it is not necessarily about the real situation, but about the way in which you see it. What happens if the threatening situation occurs? The answer is that the level of stress drops to zero! Stress is not about the here and now, most of us are much stronger than we think, we can deal with almost anything. What we can't cope with is the anticipated crisis.

What we are talking about is the way in which the individual attempts to deal with those things he believes will happen in the future. At first, we try the various coping responses that we have tried in the past. What happens if they don't work? If the old coping responses don't work, then you try other coping responses which are new, not necessarily consciously, not necessarily saying to yourself, "I think I will try a new mode of problem solving" but this is what one tends to do. But if the new coping mechanism still doesn't work, then a very interesting thing takes place. You begin to change your general behaviour. This is what is known as task oriented behaviour and you begin to use more of the channel capacity in your system to protect yourself than you do to perform your job. You begin to experience a circuit overload. So much energy is needed for you to cope with the threat that there is insufficient energy for your primary task. At this point the efficiency level drops, even below the level necessary for minimal expectations. We become so involved with our problems that we do not have enough capacity to handle the usual amount of mental or physical energy necessary to do our job properly or to solve problems that really need all the attention they can get. At this point, we begin to experience physical symptoms. We may have heart palpitations, elevated blood pressure, feelings of dread, anxiety, or other symptoms begin to appear. These of course only serve to make things worse. Since the threat may not even be a real one, it is very difficult to get rid of it and if your responses are not able to deal with it, there is continous pressure placed on the totality of the defensive system. When you are exposed to those things in the environment that you would under less stressful circumstances handle with relative ease, you are now no longer able to ward them off. For example, you are liable to catch a cold much more easily or become vulnerable to various virus or bacteria that previously you may have been able to ward off. In short, as we said with physiological stress, we become prone to what is called secondary stressors. For example, in the case of a terminal illness such as cancer, death is often the result of pneumonia. Combating the secondary illness under such circumstances is far more difficult. It is a very normal and healthy thing for our defensive system to be called into play when there is danger to the body. This is physiological stress. But the question arises, what will happen when you begin to experience these changes when you are under "psychological" or "emotional" stress. Exactly the same physical behaviour occurs, the same hormones are released, the same blood sugar is diverted, the entire body is placed on the alert. When you are frightened, worried, or anxious, you body responds in the same manner as if you were being attacked by injury, virus or bacterial infection. But in the case of psychological stress, this condition of maximum defensiveness, of alertness, continues because unlike physical stress, psychological stress doesn't necessarily get resolved. Again, as in the case of physical stress, you are subject to the harmful effects of secondary stress. At this point, you have an entrance into all of the stress diseases because these defences, if prolonged, set in motion many physical diseases such as ulcers, heart disease, diabetes and all the various other conditions that occur when psychological stress continues. Doctors believe that between 50 and 80% of all diseases are psychosomatic or stress related. Indeed, stress is considered to be the number one killer. Dr. Meyer Friedman in his book TYPE A BEHAVIOUR AND YOUR HEART tells us that both high blood pressure leading to heart attacks and strokes are the result of stress.

3

Stress in the Work Place

Certainly the work place is stressful. For many years, we thought that this condition was a special disease associated only with the people at the top. A survey in the United States showed that on the shop floor there were twice as many heart attacks reported than had occurred with the top executives. Contrary to popular belief, stress among top level personnel has been shown to be a positive factor in their lives. Somehow, they have learned how to let stress work for them rather than against them. Professor W.S. Bullough at Birbeck College, London, shows that mice whose normal life span is two years, can be made to live twice as long if they are subjected to repeated stress. This occurs because exposure to intermittent stress stimulates the adrenal glands and keeps the body's defense mechanisms working at peak efficiency. It has been discovered that a regular shot of adrenalin is also helpful in dealing with lethargy and boredom. Depression, for example is less in evidence where the individual has a tension reducer in the form of an avocation or a hobby. There is an interesting belief in psychology called the Yerkes-Dodson law. It says that anxiety improves performance until a certain optimum level of arousal has been reached. Beyond that point performance deteriorates as higher levels of anxiety are attained. Dr. Hans Selye says, "The goal is certainly not to avoid stress ... but to find your optimum stress level". Our illustration of the motor car continues to be a good one ... learn when to use first gear and also learn how to shift your body into fifth gear.

We believe that it is important to admit that you are under stress. In fact we can begin to list those things in our workplace that are stressful. Stress is brought on by a noisy environment, inadequate lighting, poor ventilation, people working too closely to each other, doing what you have to do rather than what you want to do, time pressures, performance pressures, difficult interpersonal relationships, eye strain, inadequate sleep, improper diet, excessive use of alcohol, lack of exercise, inability to relieve tension, marital conflict, financial problems, lack of recognition are just a few of the many types of circumstances that cause stress. Rather than allowing these things to take hold of you, to control you, to carry you away, it is extremely helpful if you begin to understand that they ARE stressful and think in terms of what you can do about them. Think about alternatives, think about solutions to problems, think about ways of coping. We will always have problems, we will always have stressors, but we can put forth much more effort to control the way in which we deal with them.

Positive reinforcement is a very important feature of behaviour modification. Every time you are successful, every time you do not succumb to stressors, indeed, every time you cope more effectively with stress, feel good about yourself, feel that you have taken control. This positive reinforcement is very helpful.

In using these principals specifically on the job we need to know three things (1) what is causing the stress, (2) how the stress is affecting us physically and emotionally and (3) what we can do about it. It is very important that of stress and the concept of stressors be understood by all levels of personnel. Management can profit from understanding what might be stressful to people in all departments and areas of the company. It is seen therefore as a personal and a corporate responsibility. From a personal point of view, rather than being carried away by those things that are happening to you or adversely affecting you, an analysis of the situation will enable you to take the first step. If we fail to understand the overall concept of stress, we can do nothing but experience the harmful end results of it. We can be adversely affected both physically and psychologically. Once we learn to turn off the old archaic system, we can stop the harmful effects that stress has upon us.

Learn how to verbalize our feelings appropriately. It is no good to complain about our problems or feelings to those who are in no position to help the matter. If we need to change something that is stressful, think about as many positive suggestions as possible before making a presentation to someone who has respons-ibility.

Consider those factors in your life away from work that may in fact be the real culprits. It is no good trying to blame some aspect of the work environment if the primary cause is somewhere else. Be honest with yourself in this regard. Too often we have had a poor night's sleep, an altercation with family, a bad experience on the way to work that sets in motion feelings that manifest themselves at work.

We have listed some very helpful suggestions that many people have found to be of great benefit when we consider the overall aspect of job related stress.

1. Start off your day with breakfast. Many people tell us that they are not interested in eating in the morning. We have found that only a cup of tea or coffee and a bit of toast and some fruit can make an enormous difference in the way your day can start.
2. If possible use the breakfast time if you are eating on the run to meet with friends and co-workers. Use this time to enjoy a brief period of relaxation.
3. Avoid drinking too much coffee or tea during the day. Change to water or fruit juice.
4. Organize your work by setting priorities. Try to avoid too many surprises and unexpected tasks.
5. Take notes. When you write something down, you will have less chance of forgetting. This can be extremely helpful in avoiding stress.
6. Perfection is not always a desired goal. Expect to do things less well at times. When this does occur, move on and don't dwell on the negative.
7. Do one thing at a time. Several tasks will over-tax your system and cause difficulties.

8. If possible, come into work early or stay later as opposed to taking your work home. Use the time away from the office as private time, time in which you can do other things that are also important to you.
9. Reduce the noise level. Rugs and draperies can help. This may not always be an easy thing to do, but noise is a major cause of discomfort which can be stressful
10. Restrict telephone calls by having them held over or close the door when you are busy.
11. Plan so that you can use uninterrupted periods of time for smaller jobs that need to be done.
12. You are as responsible as the next person for a pleasant work environment. You do your part to make your surroundings as stress free as possible.
13. If you are annoyed about something, tell the people who can actually do something about it. Don't hold things in. Approach the problem by using suggestions that can be positive and helpful.
14. Develop a support system. Can peak workloads be shared?
15. Don't take you job with you on your break.
16. Take a creative lunch break. Do things that need to be done, but also think about going to places near your work that you would like to see or just find a place where you can sit for a time and relax.
17. Go to lunch as often as you can with a co-worker and try to talk about things that are not work related.

18. Relax and meditate. Later on we will be sharing with you biofeedback techniques. Once you know how to use these techniques, begin to use them.
19. Develop good habits away from work such as good eating habits, habit control, such as alcohol and smoking. Chapter 6 will help you in this regard.
20. Monitor your work, rest, recreation balance. Are changes needed?
21. Consider ways you can enjoy your co-workers by planning outings, birthday parties or office parties.

We have listed some further suggestions to help you deal more effectively with stress that require more effort but will be extremely beneficial.

1. Develop a wider variety of sources of gratification in your life, your family, in your hobbies and in your interests. Plan occasional special weekends.
2. Consider changing your job or having your job responsibilities changed to better meet your interests or skills.
3. Learn how to be assertive. Learn how to express differences in feelings and attitudes. Understand that it is sometimes necessary to say "no".
4. Begin to look for emotional support from those with whom you work, your supervisors, spouse, friends and family. It is also important to be a good listener. Others will need to get support from you as well.

All of us are much stronger than we think. We have solved many problems in our life and we will solve many more in the future. Begin to develop more and more confidence in yourself and in your ability. In the workplace, begin to gain the reputation of a problem solver rather than a problem maker.

4

Stress in Interpersonal Relationships

We need so much to be accepted. We need to be liked, to be considered to be important. Because we are afraid that we will be rejected, not accepted and not loved, we are fearful. We anticipate the worst in our relationship with others. This is a major stressor.

The answer is very simple. Since we know that people need to be liked and accepted, since we know that others will need to impress us, we give them every opportunity to do so. Rather than being worried about whether or not we will be accepted, we put forth effort to role reverse. When we are with someone else, we see life through their eyes. We accept them, we like them, we acknowledge them. This will make life so much easier for everyone. We therefore abandon the need to prove ourself, to gain acceptance from others. People are not as interested in you as they are interested in their own needs.

Many psychologists will tell you that marriage as we experience it today is a very stressful institution. Over

40% of marriages today end in divorce. However, the divorce rate for people who re-marry is now up to 50% and even higher for the third marriage. Why is this? We believe that we consider only getting a legal divorce and overlooking the fact that we need an emotional divorce as well. We often enter into the second or even third marriage with many unresolved emotional problems. Therefore we are not giving ourselves wholeheartedly to the new marriage. When we have secured an 'emotional divorce' from the previous marriage, we can then move ahead unincumbered.

For the past 25 years I have been involved in clinical work of which marriage and family counseling took up most of my time. I have been asked, "Why are family relationships so stressful today?" My answer has been that people are often too selfish to consider the needs of others. What I am saying is that we are so overwhelmed with our own needs that we can not consider the needs of other members of our family. Remember, stress is about the future. It is a constant fear of what will happen. If we believe that our needs will not be met, we are in a state of constant apprehension. For any relationship to work, it must be based on a 90-10 ratio. We must be prepared to give 90% and expect 10% in return. If the other person is also prepared to give 90% and expect only 10% in return, then we are putting forth so much effort in giving our 90% that we cant't help but experience a positive relationship. When we are anticipating that things will work out well, when we believe that problems will be solved, when we are prepared to consider others before our selves, then there is very little threat or fear and as a consequence very little stress.

Life outside of the emotional relationship will present so many problems for us to solve that we need all of the energy we can muster to deal with them. But if we are using so much of our creative energy in solving our personal interpersonal relationships then there is none left over.

Over six thousand years ago, a Greek philosopher complained about the problems that existed between young people and their parents. Growing up has always been stressful. It is a time when the mind and body are experiencing major changes. If this was the case in ancient times how much more stressful it must be today. We first accept the fact that young people need to cast off their old childish value system and re-establish themselves on what to them will be a more mature adult system. In order to do this, they are inevitably going to come into conflict with their world. If we know this and can anticipate many of the things that will happen, we will then be in a better position to both predict and prepare. In all areas of stress, we will be well advised to deal with whatever happens in a straight forward manner rather than using denial. Regardless of what may happen in the way of adolescent behaviour, we must think in terms of problem solving rather than admonishing and resorting to strong emotion. In all of our dealings, whether it be with a husband and wife set of problems or with parent and child or indeed parent and the elderly member of the family type problems, we have a procedure that we recommend. We first state the problem, we accept the possibility that the problem is stressful and then we think in terms of the alternatives regarding the solution. We think of as many alternatives as possible Using logic has never been man's strong suite. The world revolves on emotion. It has been so from the beginning of time and I suspect that it will continue well into the future. If we can find a reasonable, sensible and logical solution to the problem at hand, the stress level will diminish markedly.

We would like to list some steps that will be helpful in dealing with interpersonal stress.

1. Identify the feeling. This can be anger, frustration, resentment, jealousy for example.
2. Understand the concept of stress, understand that it is the future that we worry about.
3. Consider at least five alternatives for dealing with the problem. These alternatives can be good alternatives, funny alternatives, ridiculous alternatives, insane alternatives — it does not matter — just think of alternatives. Consider each one as thoroughly as possible. Then in concert choose the most helpful procedure for solving the problem.
4. Keep the lines of communication open. Agree to talk about your feelings, about the emotions, about the results and about the things that can be done about it.
5. See the situation through the eyes of others. Role reverse, change places as it were and learn how to emphathise.

There are going to be times when the strongest of us fail. Sometimes a marriage problem can not be solved. There will be times when the communication between children and parents can not be repaired. There will be times when an elderly member of the family has experienced such a major cognative impairment that serious measures must be taken. The task is to do what we can, to do the best we can, and to realize that outcomes will not always please everyone. It is so important to keep the stress level down. It is so important to keep the negative physical and psychological features of stress from harming us.

Let me say one thing about people who are reaching the age of retirement. This poses a unique stressor. This is a time when a major change of pace is experienced. It is experienced both for the person retiring and for their other family members. It is a time of uncertainty. The word 'retirement' implies a threat or a stressor. We fear for our health and for our wealth. We anticipate problems occurring. The best counsel I can give anyone who is 'retiring' is to consider not so much as retiring but as changing their job, or their endeavour. Rather than going to the shop, the office or the workplace each day, get up at the same time, have your breakfast in the same way as you have done over the years and then go to your new job. This new job may be working in the garden, taking the dog to the park each day, building a boat or a basket — do something that will give you both physical and emotional satisfaction. Consider what you are doing as very important. In your mind see it as being as important as the job that you have just left. This will reduce your stress.

5

Stress and Psychosomatic Disorders

Why and how is stress related to our physical bodies? Statistics prepared by the Health Service in Britian indicate that the stress epidemic cost British industry more than £1 billion a year. Over 37 million working days are lost through psychosomatic illnesses. This represents 2% of the gross national product lost. Absenteeism is one of the main symptoms managers watch for. We are told that coronary heart disease, in which stress is often the major factor kills one third of men who die between the ages of 35 and 65 in Britian. Psychosomatic disorders like migraine, allergies, ulcers, asthma and back pain are often hidden signs of tension and stress. Sleep patterns are frequently disturbed because of stress. Accidents also occur as the result of stress.

With the work of Freud in the last century, we began to understand more about what he called hysterical illnesses, illnesses that were brought about by our feelings and emotions as opposed to some physical trauma or physical cause. After World War II, we began to understand more about what was then being called psychosomatic illnesses. Over the past 20 years, we have become even more specific in this regard and have looked at the external aspects of our lives to create the concept of stressors. But exactly how does this work. Whether we are talking about hysterical illnesses in the psycho-analytic sense, or psychosomatic illnesses or stress related illnesses, we need to understand, to know that it is seldom either one thing or the other. It is seldom a physical illness completely or an emotional illness alone. We have areas of our bodies that tend to give way in time of stress. If we have a sensitive area in our bodies, this can be the area that will suffer in time of stress. Back problems that can give us difficulty easily can be a point of weakness when the external pressures mount. If our nasal membrane is delicate and we tend to suffer from hayfever, if we are under stress this area may become more acute. Although this is an extremely complicated subject and the physical and emotional mechanisms involved are also complicated, it is very helpful if we understand the concepts involved. Dr. Peter Hanson in his book THE JOY OF STRESS gives us a great deal of information on the subject. He give us specific examples of the various chemical changes that take place in our bodies in relationship to those things that are happening to us from the standpoint of our external environment. He also helps us to understand how our ancient ancestors needed many of these chemical and physical changes to take place in our bodies in order to cope with the world in which they lived. That world has long vanished, but our bodies remain very much the same.

Constriction of blood vessels in our brain can cause migraine, for example when we are worried, concerned, frightened or stressed.

Since more people die of worry than they do of work, we can very easily become fatigued not because we are actually exhausted from physical activity, but fatigued because we have had to maintain the burden of apprehension.

We can not sleep at night because we are taking our problems to bed with us. In Chapter 8, we will tell you about how we can fight back against stress and dealing with the preparation for a good night's sleep will be included. The task, with headache, backache, hypertension, insomnia or any other stress related condition must first be dealt with by 'turning off the stress system'. I advise people to picture in their mind a red button that says STOP. Press this button and the body will return to the state that existed before the stressor occurred. Feel your muscles relax, think of the breathing patterns becoming more normal, think of the limiting of the energy reserve of the body being re-directed. No longer will hormones be released to divert sugar from the smooth muscles to the striate muscles — once this has been done, once you have turned off the system, you will now have the energy that you previously needed to maintain the stress system to be available to you for the task of problem solving.

6

Stress and Habit Control

In what other ways does stress manifest itself in our behaviour? Although certain 'habits' may not in and of themselves be directly related to stress, it is possible that excess in any type of behaviour can be a part of the stress pattern. For example, many people smoke tobacco because they enjoy it. Many people drink alcohol because of the many positive features associated with it. Cooking and eating can be associated with an art form. There are others who smoke more and more when they are stressed. There are those who drink to excess or eat to excess when they are stressed.

There are multi million pound industries today directing their attention towards helping people stop smoking, stop or cut down on their drinking and perhaps the largest of these industries directs its attention towards helping both men and women lose weight. Our research and years of clinical practice has demonstrated that stress is a major factor in excessive smoking, over-eating and drinking too much. We take no moral stand. If one wants to address the subect from the standpoint of understanding more about stress so that they can either stop smoking or lose weight or become less dependent on alcohol, our methods have proven to be of value.

As is the case with the modification of any behaviour that is stress related, it is important to understand how we cope with stressors often in an ineffectual manner. For example, if we are stressed and we light a cigarette, we are still stressed, we still have the stressor, the circumstances that cause stress, but we think that by lighting a cigarette, we are actually doing something about it. We have set up a pattern of behaviour which is based on a faulty basic assumption, i.e., that a cigarette will help us. There is often absolutely no relationship to the stressor and the cigarette. The fact is that we have not dealt with the problem, we have only diverted our energies elsewhere. The behaviour is reinforced time and time again until we actually believe that the cigarette helps us to cope with the stressor. The fact that the smoking sets up physical circumstances that will cause other problems both immediately and in the future is quickly and conveniently overlooked.

When we are stressed, alcohol can do a good job of covering over our feelings about our problems. In fact it often does such a good job that we don't deal with the real problem. More stress can cause more drinking which can cause more stress.

Our suggestion is initially that you make a personal determination as to what you want to do about it. It is of little or no value to stop smoking, lose weight or cut down on your drinking if you are doing it to please someone else. Although this may be a very excellent motivation, it is not sufficient for you to achieve satisfactory results. You must want to change or modify your behaviour for personal reasons. Since our suggestions designed to help you are associated with positive reinforcement behaviour modification, this aspect is of great importance. Once you have decided that you want to change or modify your behaviour, then the next step is to find a method or a procedure to do it. In conjunction with this desire to move ahead, we strongly suggest that you begin to see the habitual behavour as being stress related. Once you do this, it will make the task that much easier. Your stress card will be a great help to you. For example, you will reach for your stress card rather than reaching for your cigarette, drink or the food you don't need. Once you have been able to begin to practice the relaxation techniques on the back of this card, you will find it will take the place of your 'habit'.

Our cassette tape programmes are available to those who want to have specific help in the learning of specific techniques in the area of slimming, stopping smoking and becoming less dependent on alcohol. Although we believe that it is possible to control one's drinking, we do not believe that one can 'cut down' on tobacco. In this instance, you either smoke or you do not. We have found that it is most difficult to smoke just a few cigarettes a day.

7

Stress and Motoring

Most of us today would agree that one of the most stressful things we do is drive a car. Whether we are driving only a short distance or spending hours on the motorway, we soon discover that we are becoming tense. Often our muscles contract, our eyes become tired, we are apprehensive, we experience many typical stress or tension symptoms. This serves to limit our ability to drive as carefully as we should. It puts strain on the totality of the system. But is this a bad thing? Do we not need to be alert, to be aware of other drivers, of the road conditions, of the condition of our car and of all the other necessary factors if we are to be alert, skillful drivers. This is an example of stress being a good thing. But what happens when we become so involved in the fear, the worry, the apprehension that we limit our ability to deal with all of the driving circumstances in an orderly and relaxed manner. What we are suggesting is that we can, under difficult circumstances say to ourself, "... it is beginning to rain, the road will be wet and I must relax and pay close attention to my driving". In other words, you begin to TAKE CONTROL. Become aware of the stress and let it work for you rather than against you. You may say, "... the number of cars seem to be increasing, I must slow down and become more alert to my driving". Often, on a long journey, we note that our neck or shoulders may be stiff, we may have discomfort in our legs or arms. This is frequently the result of stress. When this happens, reflect to yourself that this is an indication of stress and begin to practice the stress reduction procedures. First accept that you are stressed, begin to relax your stomach muscles, become aware of your breathing, relax, but not to the extent that you are no longer diligent. If we properly recognize that we are stressed and as a consequence fatigued, this will be the time to stop the car, pull in for petrol or have a cup of tea or coffee.

8

Fighting back against Stress

As we begin to understand more about stress, it is necessary for us to be able to think in terms of how we can begin to let stress work for us rather than against us. It is necessary for us to begin to modify our thinking, our behaviour and our approach to life in general as we begin to fight back against the harmful effects that stress can inflict upon us. In all instances, we will continue to admonish the reader to think in terms of solving problems rather than being carried away by them. The difference between the successful person in any walk of life is that somewhere down the line there was a thought process geared toward thinking of solutions to what might have appeared to be a problem. The less successful person becomes imbroiled in the problem and is seemingly incapable of addressing the task of finding a solution. This philosophy implies that there is a solution to be found and with this attitude, the stressor becomes less powerful. Immediately we think about a positive outcome rather than thinking only of the threat.

Dr. Thomas Holmes of the University of Washington in America talks about what he calls Life Change Units. He has made a study of the effects of change on our physical and mental processes. According to Dr. Holmes "Four out of five people who have experienced many dramatic changes in their lives over the past year can expect a major illness within the next two years". He worked with the help of Richard Rahe, a medical student in setting up what is now called a Social Readjustment Rating Scale which makes it possible to estimate the degree of adaptational stress we are suffering at any given time. He found that while 80% of people with a score of over 300, and 53% of people with a score of between 150 and 300 became seriously depressed, had heart attacks or suffered other forms of serious illness. These disorders occurred in only 33% of people who scored 150. This research suggests that whenever possible we should limit the amount of change occurring during any one period of our lives. By using this scale, calculate the number of Life Change Units you have.

MEASURING AND RELATING LIFE STRESS TO PHYSICAL AND MENTAL DISORDERS

Holmes and his colleagues have developed the Social Readjustment Rating Scale, which is an objective method for measuring the cumulative stress to which an individual has been exposed over a period of time.

EVENTS:	SCALE OF IMPACT:
DEATH OF SPOUSE	100
DIVORCE	73
MARITAL SEPARATION	65

JAIL TERM	63
DEATH OF CLOSE FAMILY MEMBER	63
PERSONAL INJURY OR ILLNESS	53
MARRIAGE	50
FIRED AT WORK	47
MARITAL RECONCILLIATION	45
RETIREMENT	45
CHANGE IN HEALTH OF FAMILY MEMBER	44
PREGNANCY	40
SEX DIFFICULTIES	39
GAIN OF NEW FAMILY MEMBER	39
BUSINESS READJUSTMENT	39
CHANGE IN FINANCIAL STATE	38
DEATH OF CLOSE FRIEND	37
CHANGE TO DIFFERENT LINE OF WORK	36
CHANGE IN NUMBER OF ARGUMENTS WITH SPOUSE	35
MORTGAGE OVER £6,000	31
FORECLOSURE OF MORTGAGE OR LOAN	30
CHANGE IN RESPONSIBILITIES AT WORK	29
SON OR DAUGHTER LEAVING HOME	29
TROUBLE WITH IN-LAWS	29
OUTSTANDING PERSONAL ACHIEVEMENT	28
WIFE BEGINS OR STOPS WORK	26
BEGIN OR END SCHOOL	26
CHANGE IN LIVING CONDITIONS	25
REVISION OF PERSONAL HABITS	24
TROUBLE WITH BOSS	23
CHANGE IN WORK HOURS OR CONDITIONS	20
CHANGE IN RESIDENCE	20
CHANGE IN SCHOOL	20
CHANGE IN RECREATION	19
CHANGE IN CHURCH ACTIVITY	19

CHANGE IN SOCIAL ACTIVITY	18
MORTGAGE OR LOAN LESS THAN £6,000	17
CHANGE IN SLEEPING HABITS	16
CHANGE IN NUMBER OF FAMILY GET-TOGETHERS	15
CHANGE IN EATING HABITS	15
CHANGE IN VACATIONS	13
CHRISTMAS	12
MINOR VIOLATIONS OF THE LAW	11

For persons who had been exposed in recent months to stressful events that added up to an LCU score of 300 or more, these investigators found the risk of developing a major illness within the next two years to be very high, approximating 80%.

One of the most valuable contributions in the field of psychology over the past few decades is a device called 'biofeedback'. We use this process in helping us both diagnose and treat stress. Your stress control card is a biofeedback device.

Let me tell you something about biofeedback. Doctors have always been involved in obtaining "feedback" information each time they use a variety of instruments in assisting them in making a diagnosis. A fever thermometer or a blood pressure gauge are "feedback" instruments. Within recent years, we have combined what is known as galvanic skin response and temperature with information received from the amplification of brainwave activity to provide us with knowledge concerning our physical reactions and stress. This is called a "biofeedback monitor". On the front of your stress card, you will find a liquid crystal that will change colour depending upon the temperature of your thumb. When you are stressed, blood is drawn into the centre of your body, to your vital organs. This causes your hands to become cold and clammy. The temperature drops and this can be measured by the heat sensitive liquid crystal. If the crystal remains black, you are stressed. When the crystal turns blue, you are very relaxed. If you see that you are stressed then you begin to use our techniques for helping you to become relaxed and in so doing, you will limit the harmful effect that stress is exerting on your body.

Dr. Thomas Budzynski in America is a researcher in the area of biofeedback and has written a paper called 'Turning On The Twilight Zone'. He says, "For a brief time as we lie in bed at night, neither fully awake nor yet asleep, we pass through a twilight zone that Arthur Koestler has described as a state of reverie. Many people associate this drowsy state with hallucinatory images, more fleeting and disjointed than dreams, and compare it to the viewing of a speeded-up, jerky series of photographic slides. A host of artists and scientists have credited the imagery of this twilight state with reactive solutions and inspiration of their work". He goes on to say, "We are now beginning to understand that during this brief somnolent state, people not only may have creative insights, but may also be more in touch with the unconscious in general. They are hyper suggestible and capable of learning certain things more efficiently and painlessly than during the day, when logical and analytical faculties are in control. There is even evidence that the suspension of critical judgment associated with the usually dominant left hemisphere of the brain may allow the non-dominant right side of the brain, with its more intuitive and emotional processes, to take over".

All of our cassette tape programmes employ this "twilight learning" theory. We combine positive reinforcement behaviour modification with this theory and have received some remarkable results that are consistent with those results of the American psychologists.

In order to achieve this 'twilight state' we employ progressive relaxation. Dr. Robert Sharpe who undertook his research at Nottingham University has made a major contribution in his work which advocates the value of relaxation in order to help us cope with stress.

We mentioned earlier that meditation and relaxation are of such importance during a busy day. Now how many of you will say, "When and how will I be able to meditate in the course of a busy day?" Once you understand how it can be done in no more than a minute you can appreciate how quickly the body will respond positively to only a brief period of relaxation. By meditation, we mean nothing more than having good thoughts about what you will have for supper, what you will do on your way home or what you will do over the next weekend. I remember a clergyman once saying, "One Sunday a month, during my sermon, don't listen to anything I am saying. Use the time to think about your own personal circumstances, think about your problems, think about your holidays, use the time constructively. This will often do you as much good as the words and message of my sermon". Do we really think, and hopefully think positively about the things that need our attention. Find a few minutes each day to take out your stress card, relax and have a few minutes of constructive thinking.

Your stress control biofeeback card is a relaxation trainer as well as a stress monitor. Every time you get the card to turn blue, feel good about yourself, feel that you are in control, stress is no longer controling you.

We would like to share with you some of the ways in which we can better manage stress.

1. Improve your self image. Begin to see yourself as an important person. You are just as much entitled to a good life as anyone else. If you do well, enjoy what you have done or accomplished. If you have not done as well as you would have liked or if you make a mistake, learn from it and move on to the next situation. Don't dwell on negatives.

2. Find as many positive features as possible with those with whom you live and work. It is interesting that if we believe people will be helpful in their relationship with us, they are more inclined to be than if we expect them to be otherwise. So much stress results in our negative and fearful attitude towards other people.

3. By combining our positive self image and our positive attitude about life in general and in people with whom we live and work, it will be much easier to move forward. We can assert ourselves without being hostile or overly aggresive.

4. Improve our habits such as smoking, diet, rest, exercise and good health. So much stress is the result of just not taking proper care of ourselves and as a consequence, we produce problems resulting from our bad habits.

5. Find a tension reducer in the form of a hobby or interest away from our usual work.

6. Think about improving our verbal communication skills. Develop the ability to talk about our feelings in a positive and constructive manner.

7. Begin to TAKE RESPONSIBILITY for your behaviour. It is not helpful to blame others or find excuses for things that occur. Once you do this, you will have more positive energy available to you for the task of problem solving.

TAPPING INTO OUR SUPER POWER

Through biofeedback training and progressive relaxation, we are able to derive some very interesting results. Once we have begin to let stress work for us rather than against us, we can take the next step. We can begin to use our SUPER POWER. All of us have far more ability in both a pysical and emotional sense available to us than we realize. In the time of emergencies, it is possible to experience feats of strength that we did not think possible. Although our cassette tape programme STRESS MANAGEMENT goes into this in much greater detail, we want to point out that with stress control, we are able to use the energy previously used in having to worry so much about life that we now have this energy available for other things. We can use it for learning any new information. We can use it for increasing our powers of concentration. We can use it to improve our ability in sports and it is also possible to use it to reduce pain.

Once you have developed the ability to turn the card blue quickly, you are now able to take the next step in learning progressive relaxation which will enable you to focus all of your mental and physical energies on a specific task. Through improved powers of concentration, there is so much more in life available to you. After you have developed the ability to control stress, there is no limit to what you can do.

The most important thing that you will receive from this programme is the ability to TAKE CONTROL OF YOUR LIFE. You will be able to think positively, you will be able to think maturely and you might even begin to develop the ability to think logically. By taking control of your life, you will be in a far better position to deal with the alternatives that yield solutions to the stress you experience. When you are in control, you will not be a slave to tobacco, alcohol, drugs or will you attempt to solve your problems by overeating. You will feel very good about yourself.

9

The "Ten Step Programme"

Over the years, we have developed a Ten Step Programme for stress management. We would like to share this with you since it has been so well received through our tape programme Stress Management.

First of all, our life and our perception of it is subjective. Beauty is absolutely in the eye of the beholder. Pain and suffering is also very personal. We have talked a great deal about stressors. That which might be a threat, a forerunner of stress to one person may not be a threat to another. It may well be that what we see or hear or perceive is not in any way representative of the true picture. We must determine whether the threat is a real one or the result of a situation which we believe to be real. We live in our minds — our world is entirely of our making, of our perception. So many, many of life's experiences that we think are threatening, potentially stressful, are being viewed with so much strong emotion at the time that we may be entirely wrong about the situation. Therefore one of the initial steps is to re-think or re-appraise that which we believe to be a threat.

STEP ONE is to call the emotion by name. Say to yourself, "I am frightened, I am worried, I am angry, I am frustrated". Accept the emotion, understand the feelings associated with it. At this point, it will be helpful to realise that you are going to be able to put into practice the subsequent steps that will enable you to deal effectively with the emotion and with the thing that is causing stress. Know that you are armed and ready. Confidence will rise when you know that you can begin to cope more effectively with the emotion and the circumstances surrounding it. Once you have embarked on this step, this will be the beginning of learning how to use stress management to your advantage. In the main, most people are just carried away by stress, they don't understand and as a consequence can't let it begin to work for them rather than against them. By taking the first step, you have now set in motion a process that will lead to success in so many areas of your life. This will be the beginning of the process of taking control.

STEP TWO is called "Reality". Is the threat a real one, or is it not? Is it based on fact or on some emotional fear of the moment? It is possible to over-react to stimulus. We need to test the validity, the truth of the stressor or of the perceived stressor. For example if you are indeed frightened, or worried, determine whether or not the emotion is justified. If it is, think of the altenatives available to you for dealing with it. There is an unfortunate trap called "denial". If the threat is in fact a real one, then deal with it, don't deny it. This can be as harmful as over-reacting to what might be called a minor threat. Reality evaluation enables us to proceed with the logical problem solving mechanisms. At times there are things that are real, they are potentially difficult situations. The task is not to attempt to insure that life will have no more problems for us, but to accept them and address ourselves to the solution with maximum energy. One problem associated with over-reacting is a squandering of physical and mental energy. With an honest appraisal we can begin to use our problem solving processes more effectively. From the standpoint of denial as a coping mechanism, it is not that denial does not help us to reduce threat, the problem is that it does to a certain extent. However, it is just because it reduces the threat that it often prevents a more effective and enduring strategy from being employed. Denial is a very primitive and indeed typical behaviour used by persons who experience threat, because it works, but up to a point and it often brings additional stress with the situation ultimately. One denies reality, for instance, and later it is thrust upon us and the situation is then made worse.

The THIRD STEP is accepting responsibility for our own decisions and actions. We are threatened — we may be stressed. We must recognise that there is nothing abnormal or unusual about this. In a world in which most of the things that happen are not under our control, it is almost inevitable that we will perceive threat again and again. This is what life is for everyone. The important point is that our actions, our coping responses should make the situation better, they should reduce the threat, restore the balance. If they do, well and good, we are normal, and can face the future threats with assurance. If not, if they make matters worse and we are moving toward the abnormal when the inadequacies of our coping responses simply increase the threat. Although we are not responsible for the way we feel, we are responsible for what we do about our feelings. It is not helpful either to blame other people or contend that it is their responsibility for our problems.

The FOURTH STEP is that of releasing the tension which has been created by the stressful circumstances. This can be done both by physiological and psychological means. We suggest that you use one of our two methods for releasing tension. One is the method available to us when time is not immediately a critical factor. We mentioned the "twilight learning" technique. In order to become involved in the progressive relaxation exercise associated with this technique, we suggest that you find a comfortable place to sit down or lie down and relax. This is very helpful when you are experiencing insomnia. You will be asked to close your eyes. If you wear contact lenses, you may want to remove them. You will be more comfortable if you will loosen your clothing or take off your shoes. Before you close your eyes, it will be helpful if you spend a few seconds getting your eyes tired so that it will feel comfortable when you close them. Focus your attention on some small object in the room in front of you. Lock your eyes on this object. When it has your full and complete attention, take a deep breath, and as you let it our say, 'five, five, five' and close you eyes. Continue to count down by saying, "four, four, four, three, three, three, two, two, two, one, one, one, relax." Allow every muscle in your body to relax. One can increase the level of relaxation and diminish anxiety by imagining you are taking an escalator going down. Pretend to be stepping on the escalator going down. Imagine yourself taking hold of the hand railing. Feel the movement of the escalator going down, down, down. Allows yourself to become much more relaxed. Feel your breathing patterns becoming much easier and with each breath, allow yourself to go deeper and deeper into relaxation. It is helpful if you feel your stomach muscles relax completely. As your stomach muscles relax, feel all of the tension leave your body. Feel your stomach muscles become limp and loose. Feel all of the tension disappear. Feel your body completely relax. At this point, begin to consider your circumstances. Utilise this tension free experience for a genuine mobilisation of all of the positive factors available to you. As you take air into your lungs in this relaxed manner, become aware of the oxygen going to your brain. Know that this oxygen is helping the totality of the mental processes. Focus your attention on this experience for a moment. Feel the rythmical patterns of breathing. Picture the oxygen travelling to your brain. Begin to feel the positive effect, allow the thoughts to form, conceptualise your circumstances. Feel that you are able to address yourself to them in a more energetic fashion. Once you have completed this "twilight learning" experience you can count upward from one to five, then you will open your eyes and carry on your day. If you are practicing this process at night just before you go to sleep, give yourself the instructions to go to sleep immediately to sleep soundly all night and to awaken fresh and rested in the morning.

But what does one do when time is not available? By having previously practiced the meaningful procedure of "twilight learning", by having become so skilled in the diminishing of tension through this process of relaxation, one can now do this very quickly even without the necessity of utilising the entire procedure.

You can actually feel the tension diminish by the conscious effort of relaxing the stomach muscles, feel all of the body responding to the relaxation of the entire centre part of the body. Feel the tension disappear. Feel the oxygen going to your brain. Feel the mental processes working for you and with you. This brief experience can be enjoyed even under what may seem to be serious problems. Through this process you will know that you will be able to handle anything in a far more effective manner than by allowing strong emotion, uncontrolled, to deprive you of the mental energy available for the task of problem solving. Therefore it becomes most important that one gets rid of tension before attempting to take the other steps.

The FIFTH STEP is called the law of extinction exercise. By this, we mean a procedure by which we render less and less harmful or potentially harmful set of feelings and their consequences. We wear them out, as it were, we make them become extinct. It is not always easy to brush away fear, worry or anxiety even by a process of intellectualization. For just a moment, actually allow yourself to experience the emotion such as fear or frustration. Allow the feeling to become intense. Allow the worry or anxiety to become intense. Say it to yourself, "I am really frightened". Feel the fear mount. Feel it become intense. At this point, picture in your mind a giant ocean wave reaching its crest. At that moment, feel the emotion, allow it to become intense. Now, picture the ocean wave subside against the beach, see the ocean wave become less and less and less. Do this several times. Allow the emotion to become intense, feel your stomach muscles become tight, then, allow your stomach muscles to relax. Allow every muscle in your body to relax. This is what is known as flooding. It is also a procedure of making the emotion become extinct, allowing the emotion to build up, to diminish and to disappear.

The SIXTH STEP is called the displacement step. Picture yourself standing in a room with a balcony. You are standing on the balcony looking down into the room. Below there is a person who is attempting to solve a problem. This person is in exactly the same circumstances as yourself. You, however, are completely detached. You have displaced yourself. You can observe without being seen, but you know exactly what the other person is both thinking and feeling. Do this without your own emotions being involved. Take time to make observations of this person. See it as it were through their eyes, but without emotion. This procedure is of great value and will give you even more assistance once you have "stepped back into yourself" as it were. This will yield far more objectivity to your task of problem solving than you could do otherwise.

STEP SEVEN is an appraisal of your strengths. Evaluate your own ability to resolve your problem. Remember, you have thus far in your life experienced thousands of problem solving siutations. You have done it in the past and you will also be able to do it this time. You are far stronger than you realise. Your strengths are never utilised to the fullest. Your ability to think, to reason, to develop alternatives, to muster hidden resources are legion. You have within you the ability to handle far more in life than you think. Do not sell yourself short. Make an actual list of all your assets and begin one by one to utilise them. Begin to remember how you were able to address yourself to problems in the past and remember all of the various solutions that you were able to employ. This will be extremely helpful.

The EIGHTH STEP is to consider getting help from others. It is important at this point that you consider getting help, but once you consider it, forget it. Yes, forget it. Reject this for the moment as a step to take. All too often we admit defeat and in frustration call for help. At this point, consider many reasons why this is not the time to ask for help and then, go back to STEP SEVEN. Remember, potentially, you are stronger than almost anyone else you know. Only you are both subjective and objective. Again, re-evaluate your strengths and recall the many times in the past in which you have handled situations, doubtless many of which were worse than the present one. Pretend to be putting on a psychological suit of armour. This will give you security. See yourself dressed as a knight of old, knowing that he could face any battle because the arrows and axe blows would be fended off by his outward protection. Do this in your mind's eye. Put on your suit of armour made up of the knowledge that you have in the past been able to defend yourself and you will continue to do so in the future. Then and only then can you consider getting help.

STEP NINE is a very interesting step and one that is quite helpful. This is called the negative step. Allow this to be carried to a conclusion as well. Defuse it by being able to envisage the entire picture from the threat through to your own psychological and physiological reaction, through your own intellectual assessment, even through to the ultimate negative result, even the worst result. And then, ask yourself what you will do even if the very worst is experienced. See yourself in the worst situation. Consider what you would be able to do under these adverse circumstances. Remember, you have experienced adverse circumstances many times in the past. You have the ability to manage even under adversity. You have the power, the will, the strength to overcome adversity. You have done it in the past and you will be able to do it in the future.

STEP TEN is associated with the admonition that you remember that the threats are cognative, they are in your mind, so to speak. That is where we experience them — interpret them as threatening. A useful part of stress inoculation is the process known as rehearsal. In this step, one mentally rehearses one's own behaviour in dealing with the threat. Feeling the emotion, the fears, the despair and so on and mentally going through or rehearsing one's coping responses one by one leading to a reduction of the threatening situation or facing successfully the confrontation and dealing with any after effect. This phase of rehearsal is of considerable value in that it reduces the element of fear and uncertainty each time it is practiced. It is important that the preceeding steps should have been progressed through and that the reality of the situation should have been carefully assessed and relevant and effective coping strategies considered. The ONLY world is the one you perceive, you have perceived it, you can therefore move about in it and handle it. Rehearse, therefore, everything about the situation, good and bad. Soon you will find that you are improving your ability to handle problems. When you are actually faced with any problem, you are now more skilled in concluding it to your satisfaction. Each time you are able to accomplish your goal, each time you have been able to deal more effectively with the threat, feel good about yourself. Feel the sense of accomplishment. Clearly visualize the entire situation. Feel the emotion, see the entire picture from beginning to end. It is not helpful to use avoidance, to use denial or to become overly emotional when the threat made is only minimal. You now have coping methods that will be of great value. Always ask yourself, "Is this my problem?" If the anser is "No, it is not MY problem", then leave it alone.

10

At the end of the day, what do we mean by a NORMAL PERSON?

As a psychologist, the most frequent question I am asked is what is considered normal as opposed to abnormal behaviour. People have a need to know if their feelings, their attitudes, or their behaviours are within the bounds of what would be considered normal. In the first place, psychologists don't like to use this word because it is so very difficult to deal with. It becomes at times impossible to know what is normal and what is not normal. I tend to think in terms of a better word when I am asked to counsel people. This word is disabling. Is our behavour or are our feelings of such a nature that we are hindered from being able to maintain meaningful interpersonal relationships or of doing our job without too many problems. If we are in any way disabled, then we need to have a closer look at what is happening in our lives.

I do believe in guidelines. I do feel that it is helpful if we have some measure of structure that our lives can fit into. If we are going to aspire for as stressless a life as possible, there are certain behaviours or perhaps more specifically philosophies that will be beneficial. For this reason, I am going to list what the late Dean Carl Stolz of the Hartford Theological Seminary in America listed as the six characteristics of a normal person. As a guideline for all of us, I think that they are worthy of consideration. To limit the stress we experience, these principals will be exceedingly useful. Dean Stolz says the first characteristic is that we are engaged in a socially useful occupation. If we are devoting our time to doing those things that are outside the main stream of moral or ethical standards of conduct, we are certainly leaving ourselves open for much more stress than one would if they were doing that which is collectively more meaningful.

It is helpful to have a sense of service in our work. This can be described as the ethics of mutuality. Purveyors of disservices, fraudulent practices, questionable legality are far more stressful than those that are not. One can ask, "Is my business essential, necessary or contributive to the common good?" What I do for a living, the manner in which I conduct my business or profession or industry decides in part whether or not I am a so called normal person. Pride in one's work can provide as much positive reinforcement as anything else. This feature, as we have mentioned before, is an important part of stress management.

The second characteristic is that of being wholesomely related to other people. Not only do we have to engage in a business or occupation that is positive or meaningful, but in our association with others, we are well advised to relate in a positive or as Dean Stolz says, a wholesome manner. The art of living together or working together positively can be far less stressful than living in a disharmonious manner. Do we have the capacity to co-operate? Do we have the ability to emphathise? Can we consider other people's needs as well as we can consider our own? We need people who are individuals and who march to a different drummer. They can profit from understanding those who do not seek individuality and conversely understand those who need more structure in their lives. There is a very interesting story told about a young lady filling in an application for university. It said, "Mention qualities of leadership". She wrote, "I am not a very good leader, but I am a very good follower". The admissions department wrote to her and said their files were filled with plenty of potential leaders, but what they did need were more followers. To have a positive and balanced society, we need many types of people, but the key is to be able to work together. Stress results when we do otherwise.

The third characteristic — is one honest enough and capable enough to examine himself and improve himself. Plato said, "The unexamined life is a dangerous life". Introspection and personal inventory lets us ask ourselves if we are putting as much into life as we are taking out of it. Never fear personal improvement. It is stressful to attempt to maintain a feeling of superiority. We need very much to see ourselves as being important. We are important. We deserve to have our needs met and to be successful in our endeavours. The more we are able to communicate well with our world, to present ourselves in a positive and meaningful fashion to others, the more this will be possible. If a person is unsure of themselves they will need to erect defences which often tend to be seen by others as threatening. It is most helpful to laugh at yourself as you attempt to make improvements. Never take yourself too seriously. See self evaluation as a positive thing to do. By working as a team, we think not so much as getting what we want but to want better things for our group. This can be a good attitude and will certainly make life less stressful.

The fourth characteristic is that one has a sympathetic understanding of the situations of others. We have mentioned often the need to role reverse. We can profit from putting ourselves in someone else's place. We can profit from seeing life through the eyes of others. Quite frankly, this requires both courage and maturity. We are far less threatened if we have a better feeling from where the other person is coming from. By being unsympathetic, by failing to understand the situation of others, we are increasing our susceptibility of being stressed.

The fifth characteristic of a normal person is that we cultivate a tension reducer in the form of an avocation or a hobby. All of us can do better work when we have had a chance for a change of pace. Two doctors on the golf course commented that they were better able to provide for their patients if they have had the experience of a relaxing day out of the office. By broadening our horizons, by increasing our interests, the primary task will be far less stressful. We tend to become very myopic if our world is completely closed in by work and work alone. If nothing else is available to us, we can travel in our mind or through reading or the films. Anything that serves as a tension reducer is a genuine means by which we can reduce stress.

The sixth characteristic of a normal person, says Dean Stolz, is that we have a sound philosophy of life. Do we believe in something that can give our life and our world more meaning. Are we broad minded enough to explore our world with compassion, with tolerance and with understanding. Do we accept the need to be involved in something that is greater than we are and something that will benefit all of us. A broad spectrum of outlook can give us resources that will aid us in time of stress. We can profit from the strong belief in ourselves as well as in the belief in a system that will benefit all of us. This can be a religious organisation or a fraternal organisation. We can work for a social philosophy that enables us to become more in tune with an infinite. We will then be less likely to take ourselves too seriously. We can see the world as being greater in scope than ourselves and our problems.

We create so much of our own stress needlessly. This does not have to be the case. By understanding more about stress and how we can cope more effectively with it will enable us not only to live longer, but to get far more out of our lives and positively affect the lives of those around us.

For Further Reading

Budzynski, T.H. "**Biofeedback and The Twilight State of Consciousness**" Vol 1 Pieum 1977

Carrington, Patricia **FREEDOM IN MEDITATION,** Garden City, New York 1977

Friedman, Meyer and Rosenman, Ray H. **TYPE "A" BEHAVIOUR AND YOUR HEART** New York, Fawcett Crest Books, 1974

Hanson, Peter, **THE JOY OF STRESS,** Pan Books, London 1986

Jacobson, E. **PROGRESSIVE RELAXATION** Univ. of Chicago Press 1938

Lazarus, Arnold A. **BEHAVIOUR THERAPY AND BEYOND,** McGraw-Hill, New York, 1971

Norfold, Donald, **THE HABITS OF HEALTH** , St. Martin's Press, New York 1977

Pelletier, Kenneth **MIND AS HEALER, MIND AS SLAYER,** Delacorte, New York 1977

Pleydell-Pearce, Ivor, "**Biofeedback**", **OXFORD COMPANION OF THE MIND** Edited by Richard Gregrory, Oxford 1987

Shaffer, Martin, **LIFE AFTER STRESS,** Plenum Press, New York 1982

Sharpe, Robert, **THRIVE ON STRESS,** Warner Books, London 1978

Seyle, Hans, **THE STRESS OF LIFE,** McGraw-Hill, New York 1978